Red and Black

Oviya Thirumalai

BookLeaf
Publishing
India | USA | UK

Presentation by *BookLeaf Publishing*

Web: www.bookleafpub.com

E-mail: info@bookleafpub.com

ISBN: 9789357445832

First edition 2022

DEDICATION

To SriNidhi,

My best friend and my first editor.

ACKNOWLEDGE MENT

'Vishnu' for being the person who always has and always will bail me when I mess up.
'Mom' for always putting me first, no matter the cost, and for assuming that I'm a much better writer than I am.
'Ammu Chithi' for being my role model
'Dad' for all your confidence.

'Rida, Jasmine, Swetha, Ivy, Diana, Shivani, Nini, Sai, Aarya, Anjali, Ansari, Anthony, Azhagu and Shreyash' who have stood by me in some of my toughest years, who are always there for me.
'Aamina the child', without whom I couldn't survive a single day.
'Abhi' for being an amazing best friend and partner in crime.
'Chloe' who was the first to see my work.
'Avi' for being so encouraging and understanding.
'Varsha' Your own creations have inspired and motivated me.

'Nivedita' for being unbelievably loyal,
trustworthy and for letting me talk at you till
your ears bleed. Best friends for life buddy.
'Mary' for hands down being the sweetest person
I know.
'Sruthi' for being my first proper fan. Thank you!
'Vignesh' for being my brother from another
mother.
'Siju and Ammu' for being my extended family.

'Marchi' for being my drive, without whom I
wouldn't have written a single good poem.
'Pei' for exposing me to reality, and for being the
obstacle I needed to overcome to be a better
writer.

'Adrian Buckner' for being the best teacher a
poet could ask for.
'Deva Sir, Sangeetha Ma'am, Mrs. Rose and
Jayalakshmi Asiriye' for being amazing teachers.
'JayaKrishna Sir' for being a second father to
me.

'Wattpad' for the opportunity to write, and
connect with so many new people.
'Anna Todd' for 'After', your journey continues
to inspire me to this day!

'Dylan O'Brien, Thomas Brodie-Sangster and Kaya Scodelario' for being my anchor, lifeline and role model respectively.
'Dhanush, Anirudh and Sivakarthikeyan' for being my main inspiration to start writing stories.

s19g14o16 for everything.

Black and Red

Like the red and black stripes on your pencil
pouch,
We were once woven together,
The wild innocence of children,
Competing for marks and petty pranks,
That pouch inhaled our laughter-induced tears,
And all of our ink fights,
The number of times my hair was caught in the
zipper,
And your finger, victim to the tracks,
That pouch determined us,
After all, it was the start, and it was the end.

The darkness in the colours once was
comforting,
Now? I am scared of the dark,
The colours now seem a mockery,
For I was pulsating red, and you void black,
We had inked our names with such flourish,
Your nib pierced more than just the cloth,
It pierced a heart, that still bleeds,
If only your magical pouch carried salve….

We fought every time it went missing,
Never planned of course,

And reunited every time it was found,
Why were you so careless?
It's been years since either of us have seen it,
And I must ask,
Was that intentional.

What Once Was

Whilst the child happily writes,
The adult regretfully must dot,
Trying to relive the story once more,
Sat at bench number four,
Submerged in dark shadows,
The colours have returned...

Captured in full bloom,
Protected and Preserved,
Survived multiple decades,
A faint scent still lingers,
Romance never dies,
The bloom inspired many a poem...

Soft droplets fall,
The world pure once more,
A refreshing tenderness,
Subtle hints of a smile,
Words are useless,
When the world feels too...

Dawn is drawing near,
Secrets can't survive the night,
Life isn't for the living,
The pain of parting has slain lives,

Centuries of the same story,
But our part has come to an end...

We are living our final chapter.

Solo

In my area of control,
Where breeze takes over,
And my fears melt away,
Clouds are my blanket today,
Whether the sun dips down,
Or the rain descends,
I am powerful solo.

Reborn

Leaving the blues behind me,
Driving towards the light,
For once music isn't blaring,
Yet I don't feel empty,
Rising from the grey ashes,
A phoenix blazing, red as the new sun.

Stalled

Stuck in traffic,
Having watched the emerald blush,
Trapped in the middle,
Blinking slowly with my feet,
Fighting my inevitable downfall,
Sirens call me leftwards,
And Ice cream is right,
Why do I stall like this?
Unable to let go, Unable to hold on,
Alternative routes; Alternative lives,
BEEEEP!!!
My window closed,
It's almost suffocating now,
My choice stolen by an impatient society.

Your Name

I'm in love,
Why else would the clock read three?
Blessed by the angel's touch,
To see the dawn crack,
Gazing unto a Crystal City,
Constellations form in my tears,
Happy with my life,
Sorrows finally paid their dues,
Wait.
Spoke too soon,
Stay with me. Please.

Withering Game

Well, I'll be damned,
It was but a plastic love,
Once a chirping sparrow,
I'm now a midnight joke,
The eight sags and snaps,
Your telephone number blocked,
Wind steals my fire,
Oh no. Oh yes.
I shall become a poet,
Another midnight pretender.

Peripheral

Hands shoved into a hoodie,
No vulnerabilities bared,
Wrapped in an appropriate blanket,
Seeking the secrecy and comfort of one's own
room,
Each lost,
Lost in thought, Lost in the world,
Flickering emotions only when,
The lonely bench is lonely no more.

Unspoken

I've been trampled all my life,
Behaviour dictated; Opinions influenced,
I know not who I was,
Nor who I am,
Will I even be my own entity?

Perhaps merely a clone,
A machine to be tinkered with,
Repaired and Updated,
Whenever my personality persists,
A number to the Overlord,
A letter to my fellow minions.

My name holds no value,
True meaning to be forgotten soon,
As the days of men fade,
An urge to break free,
To run away from the family,
And the ones I kid myself to believe,
Friends who are real.

I prefer the company of the strange,
Each fleeing, Each living,
A life that is secret,
A soul to be guarded,

A story still being written...

I need not to travel,
Or adopt a masked appearance,
But the freedom,
To speak as I write,
Messy, Chaotic, Brutal but Real.

End Game

His heartbeats drowned in the clock's scream,
I'm impatient to make the final moves,
Murky blue peeps out of the grey streaks above,
Brown tornadoes swirl beneath me,
A nervous cough shatters the silence,
His eyes are foolishly wet,
I inhale the fumes from our flaming field,
A wry smile crosses my lips,
Pitiful yet Predictable,
How shall I end this world?

A boxed Jack paled in comparison,
To the sweating pawn in front of me,
A little nudge is all it took,
I've dangled the bait,
Now let him bite,
Hooked, he grasps for a short-lived victory,
Incompetent to the last.

I end the war,
Striking him down,
There's a stride in my walk,
As I exit the ground,
I need a challenge,
Something to help me grow,

The battle was won too fast,
Disappointing.

Clenched fists and Forced congratulations.
Camera flashes and Featured covers.

Who cares for the king,
When he lives in a box,
His reign thwarted
Before the crown touched his head,
But why should I care about the king?
When it is the queen who slayed

Flooded

Stuck in a Hurricane,
Lost at Seas,
Forests Burn around me,
Hair-whipped by the wind,
All I need is to Stay Alive

Now or Never

Name calling and pushy demands,
Misplaced blame and petty commands,
Is this what I want?
Is this what I deserve?
I'm not your obedient servant,

This can't be real; it can't be true,
I know him well,
So what'd I miss?
Where did it all go wrong?
Just let him return, That would be enough,

Meanwhile this has to stop,
I need to take a break,
But what comes next?
On a roller-coaster with no stop,
Should I just wait for it to end?

No! I'll do it myself,
A man has no control over a woman's narrative,
History has it's eyes on you,
But I'll be writing the story of tonight,
For the first time in months, I'll actually be
satisfied,

Woman aren't helpless,
I'm saying no to this non-stop abuse,
Brush my fingers in your hair,
Kiss you one last time,
Before I take my shot.

Sparked

I craved the warmth,
The passion; The light,
Of a raging fire,
One that'd protect me,
From the wild wild world,
That'll entice me with the colours,
captivate me with the dance,
One that'll welcome me home,
And shine through the darkest of nights,
The promise of an adventure,
Of heath; Of heart; Of Hope.

I hadn't realised the irony of it all,
Fire had become my downfall,
Look closer into the flames,
Dance is but a distraction,
A gimmick to mask the agony,
Of the withering brutal murders,
Light does not lead nor guide,
but rather blinds,
Warm from a distance,
Scalding up close,
Deadening if touched,
The beasts have grown smart,
Claiming this new found weapon,

It's their home now,
Just as it were his...

Realism

Plugged in, Tuned out,
Palms Soft, Fingertips rough,
Walking alone, Thousands of friends,
Heads down, Noses Raised,
Friends lost, Networks detected,
Status updated, Secrets grown,
Tweets increased, Conversations decreased,
Realism alive, Romance dead.

Faded

I can feel myself fading away,
Slowly bit by bit, day by day,
Mind plunged into darkness, heart shattered and
voice trampled down,
Things so bad, needed to breathe fresh air in a
new town,
But did I let the good things last?

Of course not, I walked into trouble fast,
I fought and fought until I was out of fight,
I walked out of darkness into blinding light,
Connections severed, respect denied, faith
misplaced,
A happy daydream, turned living nightmare was
what I faced,

I thought I'd finally caught a break,
Little did I know, my sanctuary was fake,
I was cold too long, I guess I craved the fire,
Seeking out truths in the words of a liar,
It burnt like poison, slowly and then all at once,
And I was regretting it within months,

I remember fighting to be heard, fighting to be
free,

I was fighting to be allowed to be just me,
All this fighting, now makes me sound brave,
But in reality, all I really did was cave,
Only in my head, could I hear my own voice,
Because outside, it was drowned out in all the
noise,
From my friends, family and fashion,
To my past, plans and passion,
I was forced to admit they were all wrong,
And the list of sins I'd committed long,

I'd just resurfaced, for a breath of fresher air,
But I was dunked right back under, filled with a
growing despair,
I'd lost the best years of my life,
Became acquainted with pills, streams and
knives,
Sleepless nights from either tears or long calls,
Eventually I went numb, escaping within my
own walls,
Despite the pain being a constant but slow burn,
rather than a sharp sting,
My arms felt shackled, although it was a single
thin ring,

The screaming, the swearing, the blood,
I try hard, but memories continue to flood,
I'm lost,
My spirit stolen by a ghost,

There are some monsters you can never outrun,
And this is one,

My identity was stripped right from the core,
I stayed though, allowing it to happen more,
Now I think about it, I was nothing more than a
fool,
But isn't love the best tool?

I've withdrawn from the world outside,
Whatever is left of me, screams to hide,
I've slipped out of the grey-scale,
And the colours are returning to my life,
although still pale,
But an irreversible damage has been dished out,
Which I can never make others understand, even
if I shout,
But that is okay,
Because right now, I need to define myself to me
first, before I fade away

She pulled off her hood

She lowered her hood,
Wind thrashed against her from the edge of a cliff where she stood,
Her tears were lost in the pounding down of the rain,
This miserable loneliness which envelopes her somehow soothes her pain,
Her memories keep attacking her in flashes like the lightening,
The thundering rumble of her conflicted emotions is no longer frightening,
She lets her hoodie slip off her shoulders onto the cold hard land,
Her trainers and socks follow suit, her toes directly stand in the grassy sand,
She undoes her plait, letting her hair finally be free,
Immediately and almost violently her hair tries to flee,
She closes her eyes then opens them once more,
She was not going to allow herself to be blind like she had been before,

No longer did she need some man to help her
through the storms,
The burning need to leave, would keep her
warm.

Ventimental

I will one day be a crazy woman,
With boxes of bus passes, movie tickets and
rings,
Gum wrappers, lost marbles and CDs,
Not to mention, the trapped world,
Each lost in an infinite white whirl,
Old school timetables, vandalised by a colourful
youth,
And pristine glass bottles,
Shrouded in black and red,

But there will be one cloth bag,
Hidden away in the shadows,
Pushed out of sight; Pushed out of mind,
Once the colour of a promised pearl,
Now one of the fifty shades,
Sullied by time and tales,
Darker than a brewing stormy sky,

It'll hold my heart,
Keeping me alive forever,
Trapped in an eternal limbo,
Of Death, Life, Love, Hate, Pain and Happiness,

Words careless spilt,

Choices naively made,
Black ink diluted by the salty paper,
Titled scrawls, Jilted brawls,

My poetry will define me,
Aeons after my being burnt,
Messy thoughts finally connected,
Angry ripples find their peace,
Truth finally discovered,
I was never a villain, but the victim.

One Reason

A whirlwind of emotions,
Leaves me rattled to my core,
What sad Hell is this?
That I've fallen for?
If only I had the option of a tomorrow,
I wouldn't have to expose myself,
To the loneliness within,

A choice, A reason, A word,
It'll change my always and my forever,
Will I prosper and bloom?
Or wither with hatred?

Infused

Must I be cheerful?
Must I have a bucket list?
Must I have that special friend?
Why is happiness a side effect of dying?

Our days are all numbered,
I am no different,
Except for the occasional reminder set in my
core,
Reminding me I have but less than 365 days,
But then again, so could you,

I spend my days in bed,
Or staring at the window, music blaring behind
me,
Editing clips to make fan edits,
How does this scream depression,
When everyone does the same?

I live normally, reading and sleeping,
I live normally, binging and eating,
I live normally, learning and walking,
I live normally despite my draining health,
I am normal, despite my impending death,

Infused with intelligence, Pumped with passion,
Dripped with dreams, Treated with triumph,

Death is not a lover, but a heartbreak,
Not for those left behind, but for me now,
My concert is becoming a school talent show,
The red is turning black,

I want to make a mark,
Not because I am dying,
But because I will die as me,
Die as I lived,
Never a pretence, Never a show,

My story may never be read,
Or adapted for the masses,
Nor will I leave a legacy behind,
In fact, I will be forgotten,